Foreword

Pulling together over 60 years of recruitment experience we have compiled ... believe is 'The Best' interview guide around. We hope it is the only interview guide you will ever need…

The guide is a step-by-step; teach yourself interview skills instruction manual.

It covers and helps you answer common questions such as:

What are your weaknesses?

Where do you see yourself in 3 years' time?

It also shows you how to prepare for competency / behavioural based interviews where you are asked to describe a situation in which you have been for the interviewer to gain evidence of your competency and ability in an area. Questions such as:

Can you give me an example of when you have delivered excellent or outstanding customer service?

Competency interviews are becoming far more popular and to help we have listed the most common competency based questions asked by interviewers.

We also cover 'value based' interviews used within the Charity / Third Sector and show you how to prepare for unstructured interviews such as CV interviews.

In addition we look at telephone / video / Skype interviews, Strength and Portfolio based interviews.

The key to a good interview is to try and predict as many questions as possible, and then prepare answers to those potential questions in advance. As part of this guide we teach you a simple technique to help you predict such questions and show you how to structure answers.

We also give you over 250 interview questions with advice on how to answer them.

Highly practical in nature, this is a guide you will keep in a safe place 'just in case'.

Contents

Interview preparation

Overview

When you get an interview you have got the job!
You now have an hour to talk yourself out of it

An interview is a two-sided process. In the same way you are trying to impress the interviewer, the interviewer is also trying to impress on you how good their job is.

The second is that you would not be sat in the interview if the person seeing you did not think you could do the job. Why one person gets the job rather than another is not just down to skills and experience, it is also how well you present yourself on the day, and how you bond with the interviewer.

How well you present yourself can be easily influenced by good preparation.

Most interviews last one hour, but in effect there are only 40 minutes of actual interview. The first ten minutes is settling you down, walking you to the interview venue, getting you a drink. The last 10 minutes are taken up by you having the chance to ask questions, and being escorted from the building. So the time you have to really sell your skills, experience and demonstrate cultural fit is 40 minutes.

Preparation is the key to a good interview and it is important to remember that first impressions are very important.

Practice is also important, if offered an interview which really is not *you*, it may be worth going to the interview for practice and to try out your interview skills.

Most common reasons why people don't get the job

A survey published in The Times Career Section (Peninsula) of 937 employers highlights well the point just made about appearance. When asked the main reasons why they turned down interviewees, the main reasons were:

25%	Inappropriate Dress
20%	Unenthusiastic
12%	Bad Manners
9%	Ill Prepared
8%	Salary Obsessed

So 74% of people rejected and what is interesting is that it does not include: can't do the job or not enough experience.

So if you learn to dress yourself, say 'that sounds good' in the interview, research the company, try not to spit on the floor and don't mention money – you've got the job! If only it was that easy.

Logistics – getting there on time

The first step, once the interview is confirmed, is to look at the logistics and work out how you will get there, how long it will take, and the best means of transport. Turning up late gives a bad impression despite genuine excuses.

Also, bear in mind that most interviewers interview back to back. Just because you arrive 15 minutes late does not mean that they will make the next candidate wait. They are far more likely to cut your interview short, and when you only have 40 minutes to impress the interviewer, this could easily be reduced to 25 minutes. How many questions might they miss out?

It is not just the bad impression you are making, the interviewer may also be thinking 'If they can't get here for the interview on time, how often will they be late for work?'

So start by making sure you allow for the unexpected traffic jam, the bus not showing up. We suggest getting to the venue at least 30 minutes early. You can pay a quick visit to the toilets to check your hair, straighten your tie, or clean the mud off your shoes. But above all, you are in the building in time for your interview.

What to wear

25% of people are rejected in the survey for being inappropriately dressed.

For all interviews we recommend turning up smart. Wear a suit and tie or smart business dress if you have it, or if not, a clean shirt or blouse and smart trousers or skirt. Even if applying to a company with a 'dress down' culture or in a warehouse, going smart it sets a good impression.

If possible, no jeans, these should be the last resort. There are a few exceptions however such as if you are applying for a cleaners job or in a trendy clothes shop.

Your initial interview might be with a Recruitment Agency and so you might think 'they are only going to register me, not so important to get dressed up for them' WRONG. Having run agencies for many years the consultants will look you up and down and try and picture where they can use you. Dirty jeans, stains on your blouse or shirt, unshaven, hair a mess and shoes last cleaned at the turn of the century are all things that go against you. So even if applying for a summer job, turn up smart.

Ask yourself in advance:

- Do you need a haircut?
- Are your shoes clean?
- Is your shirt or blouse ironed:
- Are there any stains or marks on your clothes?
- Men – do you need to trim your beard or have a shave?
- Do you smell?

Sorry to be so personal with the last point but I often rejected industrial workers from jobs because of BO. After all, although working in a manual role, you need to be hygienically clean enough to sit in the break room with other workers.

Individualism need not be quelled, but some simple dress tips we would offer:

- If you wear a lot of rings and jewellery, as these can distract the interviewer, it may be helpful to take some off for the day. You want them to listen to you not spend their time looking at your jewels
- Piercings can have the same effect, depending on the role you are applying for, may wish to remove eye rings or nose studs
- Plunging necklines and short skirts on a woman may attract the male interviewer but a female interviewer may gain a totally different opinion of you
- Tattoos can put some people off employing you. They have in recent years become common place with David Beckham and pop stars leading their popularity. But even so for some roles your smart appearance is key and tattoos are a definite put off. Tattoos on your arms such as 'sleeves' can go either way with your interviewer, so think possibly about wearing a long sleeve shirt

Subconsciously, an interviewer may compare you to a stereotype or pre-judge you on your appearance. It is therefore worth considering conforming to more usual or expected dress codes when attending an interview.

Are there times when you might go to an interview more casually dressed? Yes. An engineer might be tested on the job by being asked to use a machine. If this is a possibility, take a change of clothing with you but if not clearly stated, turn up smart.

Company research

For most people:

> Preparation = Company Research
> **WRONG**
> It is just a small part of preparation

Company research is only a small part of preparing for an interview.

It can take anything from a quick review of a website to several hours surfing the web. You can use older methods such as simply telephoning the company's switchboard or customer services department and ask for a brochure or ringing the receptionist for more details, but nowadays the internet is the place to start.

Remember – If you don't have Internet access free access is available in Libraries.

If you have a laptop or other internet ready device but no internet access at home lots of retailers provide free Wi-Fi and access to the internet.

So start your research by logging into the company's website. If you are not sure what it is phone their switchboard and ask for the address. Alternatively, use Google or another search engine and search for the company there.

Now you are on their site start by looking at and making notes on:

- What they do / sell / provide
- Do they have any subsidiaries / are they part of a group?
- Are they local / national / international?
- Approximate size
- Is there a company mission statement?
- Do they have a 'values' statement highlighting their values and ethos? (it's critical you look at this if applying to a charitable based organisation)
- Who are the management team?

One of the best places to look is the 'News Release' section. In there you will often see bulletins about new products, new appointments, and lots of facts that can be used to impress an interviewer.

Next 'Google' the company under a general search and see what appears in the results. You may find articles about the business or be taken to their Facebook, Google+, LinkedIn or Twitter accounts.

And this is the next stage – you may personally hate social media but employers are being driven to it in order to promote their services and products, posting updates and tweeting about topical issues. So you next need to search social media channels for details on the company to gain more facts.

Then there is your interviewer. You should also try to research your interviewer. By entering their name into Google you may discover facts about them. These facts can be useful and by dropping in reference to them during your interview you are sure to impress them with the depth of your research. Often articles they have written can be found in the search results or even pictures of them. The more senior a person is, the more likely they may have information about them on the Internet. LinkedIn is a key tool in researching your interviewer. By opening a free account and entering their name into the search box you can often see their whole profile – CV in reality.

You can spend hours on research, but the trick is to get a basic understanding of the business and learn the odd fact so when they say 'What do you know about our business?' you have something meaningful to say. But don't get carried away. An interviewer will not expect you to have memorised the background to the company, its share price and who the main shareholders are unless you're applying for an FD role when you will also need to try and get hold of the companies' accounts.

For more senior roles, new graduates and sales people you will also need to research the industry sector, or issues relating to their business. Graduate entry schemes often have a telephone pre-screen and a common question that is asked is 'who would you see as our main competitors and why?' If they are an international firm, you will need to be able to answer this question at both a local and international level.

Sales and senior management candidates are often also asked about who the competitors are, and in particular what you see as their USP (unique selling point) or market edge the company they are applying for has. So once you have established the products or services the company sells: Google those products you find; who the competition might be; and then research these organisations also.

Marketing people may also be asked for their views on the current website design or social media presence, so in this case, don't just collect facts off the website and social media, critically evaluate the company's and their competitors' efforts also.

Company research – social / public / charity sector jobs

Company research needs to be widened even further if applying for jobs in the public, charity, environmental or other similar sectors. Interviewers will often question you on wider issues affecting their industry; bringing in political issues, legislative changes, and public opinion.

For instance, if you are applying for a teaching job, you will be expected to have an understanding of current issues both political and others effecting education in the UK. It is common for Head Teachers to include questions about your views on educational reform and changes.

Applying for a Housing Officer role you might need to research recent legislative changes in benefits or political issues affecting the sector.

If applying to a charity you will need to understand their 'values' very clearly as these will often form the basis of the interview, such organisations often using 'value based' interviews. We will cover value based interviews later, but these questions are about your own personal values and how they match the business values.

Use the printer

One trick to impress the interviewer and potentially cut down the number of questions you are asked about the company is to print off pages from a company's website and take them with you to the interview in a folder.

When asked 'what do you know about us?' open up your folder and take out the sheets showing them to the interviewer. Many interviewers are tricked by this and will assume you have read them and will only ask basic questions about their organisation as a result. The fact you have printed off the sheets demonstrates that you have done some preparation, so hit the print button at least, but be prepared for interviewers who may want to know what you have learned from the website and your research.

Print off a copy of your CV

While you are printing off pages from the website, remember to also print off a copy of your CV, the one you applied to the job with, along with a copy of the original advertisement. Take both to your interview just in case they have forgotten to print off your CV.

We say 'the CV you applied to the job with' as for your CV to gain most impact, it must be tailored to the job role applied for. Your CV nowadays may be initially read by recruiters in their first screening in less than 15 seconds. A recent survey in The Times stated teenagers' CV's are read on average in 8.8 seconds.

So a simple job hunting tip is to make sure your CV has been tailored to the job advertisement. This will help you achieve the greatest impact and will help you get through the initial screening.

A simple philosophy we promote to all our job hunters is to regard:

The Job Advertisement as an Exam Question
Your CV as the Written Answer Paper
An interview as the Spoken or Oral Exam

Analysing a role

Get into the head of the recruiter

One of the tricks to doing well in an interview is to try and predict potential interview questions in advance and prepare answers for them.

To help with this we provide in the guide some of the most common questions that interviewers use.

It is also important to identify potential skill and experience based questions in advance.

By knowing what skills the interviewer might focus on, you can start to predict likely questions. If you know what the likely questions might be, you can prepare answers for these questions.

We will now guide you through a very simple method of analysing the information you have regarding a job role such as the advertisement, job description, person specification or information pack. This technique should help you in most instances identify certainly some (if not all) of the job skills and experience requirements (competencies).

This technique works with all job types. It is based on mind mapping.

Example – post room operative

Job advertisements / descriptions / specifications are written in such a way that the most important skills and experience requirements are at the top or start.

When most people read the information they read it but don't digest or analyse the information effectively. By reading the information you have carefully, you can pick out key phrases, experience and skill requirements. By thinking about what each word means and interpreting them you can start to get into the head of the recruiter and thus start to identify what skills they are looking for and potential questions they might ask. By also thinking about 'you' in the role you can start to identify the questions.

For example – below is the first third of an advert for a post room role:

> *A fantastic opportunity has arisen for an experienced and well-organised administrator to work with a well-respected international company.*
>
> ***Job Description***
>
> *To deliver internally all incoming mail and deliveries within the buildings.*
> *To carryout scheduled collection of mail from agreed locations within the building for sorting for further distribution both internally and externally.*
> *For ensuring that mail is sent out externally using least cost routing by utilising all of the available distribution methods.*

Let's now start to analyse what seems a straightforward advert and interpret it.

Before the advertisement starts the recruiter has identified two key skills:

> *A fantastic opportunity has arisen for an **experienced and well-organised administrator** to work with a well-respected international company.*

In the first sentence they highlight that the candidate for the role needs to be:

> well-organised = Have good organisational skills
> an experienced administrator = Have administration experience

So from this you can start to predict interview questions already. Likely questions in an interview would be:

> Can you give me an example of where you have had to organise and prioritise your workload and how you went about ensuring all the tasks were completed on time?
>
> or
>
> Can you tell me about your administration experience and what types of duties you have undertaken?

If we read on:

> ### *Job Description*
>
> *To **deliver internally** all incoming mail and deliveries within the buildings.*

So the role is delivering mail and deliveries around the building. Think about what this actually involves and the skills / requirements attached to it.

First, you are representing the post room and so how smart and presentable you are at interview may be important. Second, you will be moving possibly heavy items and so may need to be physically fit. Third, you will be interacting with people and may need good communication and interpersonal skills.

It is this last point that is most important. There will be nice people, difficult people, and miserable people potentially. By walking into their departments you will need to be able to interact with them all. Therefore interpersonal skills are important.

Interviewers are likely to ask questions to see how good you are with people, but unlikely to ask you questions relating to how you get on with nice people; they will tend to focus upon difficult interaction.

Questions used to find out if you are good with people are often around winning individuals over such as:

> Tell me about a difficult person you had to win over?

or

Can you give me an example of a strong business relationship you have had to build up, and tell me why building such a relationship was so important?

Or they may focus on where you have delivered good customer service to individuals in the past. The people you will be meeting will be expecting positive interaction and good customer service from you as you deliver their post.

Can you give me an example please of where you have delivered outstanding or exceptional customer service?

In addition the interviewer may also add into the interview situational based questions (covered later in the guide), to gain further evidence based upon the competencies:

The post has left for the evening, and an important manager comes to you asking for an urgent parcel to go out that evening. How would you handle this situation and what would you say?

Reading on:

> *To carry out scheduled collection of mail from agreed locations within the building for* **sorting** *for further distribution both internally and externally*

The next sentence starts to build upon the requirement for organisational skills. It is now not just delivering the mail, but also sorting it = organisational skill.

> *For ensuring that mail is* **sent out externally using least cost routing by utilising all of the available distribution methods**.

This last sentence introduces new skills. The person needs numeric skills to be able to work out the cheapest way to send mail and parcels.

This sentence also helps define the interpersonal skill requirement and the need to build up relationships with external postal carriers.

Simply highlighting each of these skills has identified several potential interview areas:

Organisational   Administrative   Interpersonal   Numeric

So in preparing for the interview the trick is to think of questions an interviewer may ask you with regards each of the areas and prepare answers.

A technique we find works very well is to transfer this information to a visual diagram based on mind mapping techniques.

Starting with a clean sheet of A4 or larger paper if available, draw a circle in the middle and write 'Post Room' – the job title in this case. Next work through the advert or information slowly and as you identify each of the main skill or experience areas place each into a radiating circle. Linked pieces of information can be added to established facts as below:

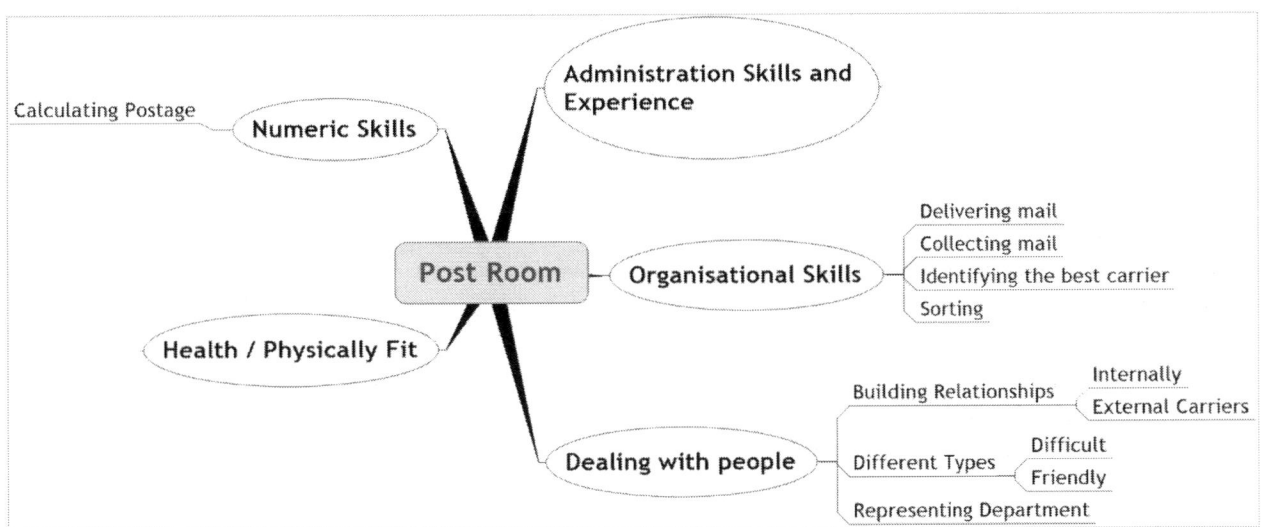

By transferring the information you are analysing it, linking relevant facts, and building up a better picture of the role requirement.

It is also important to think around these areas and interpret as well as record the facts. For instance in the Mind Map we have added to 'dealing with people', 'Different Types – Difficult and Friendly'. Thus it focuses you upon another area of potential questioning – how you deal with difficult people or build strong relationships.

You can also start to prioritise these skill requirements. If you are producing the diagram on paper, we would also recommend circling each area such as 'organisational skills' each time it is mentioned, highlighting greater importance.

People tend to repeat important things with the more times it is mentioned usually implying increased importance of that skill. With this role these are two clear skill areas of most importance; Organisational skills mentioned most, people / interpersonal skills second.

You may ask – Where does it actually highlight the need for people skills above in actual words? It doesn't... But by getting inside the role / advert, interpreting it and analysing it, you have identified a key area of skill requirement and potential area of questioning.

Interview types

There are several types of interview used by employers to select candidates. We are now going to look at each type of interview in turn suggesting how to approach each type.

You may not be sure if you are going for a 'chatty' interview or a competency based one, so our advice is to prepare for a competency based interview, the answers you prepare can be used for a whole host of non-competency questions in-order to strengthen your answers.

Remote and screening interviews

Telephone interviews

Over 50% of employers in a CIPD survey stated that they now use telephone interviews as a pre-screen.

They fall into two types, the motivational screening interview where the interviewer asks you questions about why you applied for the job, your motives for applying, and to try and get a feel for you as a person.

The second and most common is the competency based interview – the interviewer asking you for examples to demonstrate your ability and experience (covered later in this guide).

Typically these last an hour and are very 'direct' in nature. The interviewer will jump straight into questions relating to the role with little preamble. They will be writing down or recording what you say, and probably scoring your answers.

They will also be judging not just your experience, but also how well you are able to convey ideas and communicate over the phone.

To prepare for them read the section later on competency based interviews. The simple trick is to predict the questions and prepare set answers, which can actually be written down and read out as questions are asked.

Treat these as full blown competency based interviews and prepare for them as such, writing out examples to provide to evidence your ability.

The trick is to write in a thick felt tip pen each questioning area / skill area identified at the top of each sheet (so you can read it at a distance). Before your telephone interview, spread the sheets on the floor in front of you. During the telephone interview and as the topic area is raised, pick up the sheet, and use it as a crib sheet to help you describe your example.

For both types of telephone interview try and book a time when the children will not be screaming in the background, the TV blaring away, and other distracting background noise may be present. Go into a separate room so you can really concentrate and take any notes with you.

Skype interviews

Skype interviews are increasingly being used at all levels of recruitment. The disadvantage for you if you are being Skyped is that the interviewer can also watch your body language, to a limited extent.

You may be asked to a company's premises and Skyped there, but most Skype interviews are carried out at your home.

For these interviews prepare for competency based questions (covered later), and also practice in advance using Skype.

Practice using Skype is important so you are used to the technology but most of all, so you can have guidance on how you look and act on Skype. By moving your head quickly the picture blurs, by not looking at the screen you look distant, and if the lighting in the room is wrong, you can look like Uncle Fester from The Addams Family. Practice also tests your internet connection.

On the day ensure you are smartly dressed. If wearing a suit, remember to put on the trousers to match, very embarrassing if you have to get up to answer the door and still have your shorts on.

Also if others are using the internet connection at your home, ask them to log off for the duration of the interview.

Because the other person can only see you, you can have prepared examples to potential questions littered around the screen on post-it notes. However, make sure you are not obviously reading them by focussing upon them for protracted periods of time.

Graduate video interviews

A recent introduction to graduate recruitment is, forgive the expression, where you do a video 'selfie'.

Instead of an interviewer ringing you up or Skyping you, you are asked to log into a website and asked to answer set questions, your answers recorded via the camera on your device. Often there is a time limit of 60 seconds for your answer.

We presume human beings then review the videos later.

If you want to get an idea of the questions in advance these can usually be found on the graduate and student whistle blowing sites such as TheStudentRoom.co.uk, WikiJobs.co.uk, or if not in the UK their international equivalents.

The trick to get through this mechanical stage is to try and find the questions on these sites in advance. Next research the questions, and then practice on Skype with a friend delivering your answer. Most are using one minute time slots for your answer, so practice delivering your answer in that time frame.

As with Skype interviews, post-it notes with key facts dotted around the screen can be used as prompts.

Face to face interviews

CV interviews

Talk me through your CV…

This question is the basis for what is known as a CV Interview. These are not as common as an interview tool as they used to be, but are still widely used. An Interviewer is looking for a BRIEF summary of your career and work history, although inexperienced interviewers often use the question in the hope of filling time.

Most interviewers are trying to identify how your experience would be relevant for their job role, and whether they feel you would fit into their company. They are also potentially looking at personal motivators and traits.

To prepare for these interviews, first identify the main skills and competencies required by the role applied for (we suggest using the Mind Mapping technique as mentioned earlier). Now review your CV and think of how these skills have been developed or learned in different roles you have held.

If you are clever, you can as part of talking through your CV start to highlight how you have developed skills relevant to the role applied for. This needs to be subtly done so as not to sound too contrived, but if done well can really highlight how you have good skills and experience for the job role applied for.

For example for a role requiring good people skills:

'I moved to JBS because I have always like dealing with people, and in my previous role I was stuck in an office on my own. The job was working on the counter dealing with customers face to face and over the telephone. Customers would come in and I would price up their orders and then pull out the stock from the back. I really enjoyed my time there. I built up good relationships with some of the main customers.'

Now although it sounds above like a simple recounting of what the person did, in reality how the role is being described has been focused upon the people skills and how you build effective working relationships.

As part of the answer, interviewers may also want to hear about you as an individual and how you have developed your career.

Above all, when preparing your CV talk through, try and summarise your career rather than bore your Interviewer.

As you go through your CV they may ask questions around why you changed roles, look at whether you were working to targets, part of a team, working under pressure; so think about each role in relation to potential competency based questions also.

One area you really need to focus upon is why you changed jobs. This can be a real interview loser. For instance 'There was no progression opportunity so I moved to...'

What prospects exist for the new job? If none, this might imply you will be looking to move on quickly again.

Also try not to refer to old employers in a negative way.

Group interviews

As the name implies, you are asked to a group interview where you and several other applicants are brought together. As a group you will be asked to possibly carry out a group task or discuss a subject area. These are mini assessment centres.

Normally you will also be asked to introduce yourself, so practice a short introduction about your background. Often for these introductions you are asked to include an unusual fact about yourself, so think of what it could be in advance, or for your 'claim to fame'.

From the moment you are in the building you are being judged and by standing off to one side on your own you are not creating a good impression. So try and engage with other candidates by preparing in advance 4 or 5 questions to ask to start conversations. If you choose someone to talk to who is a 'brick wall', make an excuse to get away from them to get a biscuit, cup of tea, and then move to someone else to talk to.

Questions can be: 'Where are you from?' 'What are you doing currently?', if a graduate role 'Which University are you at?' 'Why did you choose that course?' 'Do you do any sports?'

During the activities remember to speak up and actively participate. Often group interviews are looking for stronger characters and confident individuals. The focus is all about how you interact with the other people.

In these interviews you may be asked questions but in the main you are taken to one side for an individual interview.

Panel interviews

A panel interview is where you face a group of people asking you questions rather than just one interviewer, and they can be quite daunting.

Usually, one person will ask all the questions, but you may find all of them throwing questions at you. The interviews are often competency based so prepare for them as we suggest later.

When being asked questions, address your answers to the person who asked the question, but make sure that you look at each of the individuals present. As a rule of thumb: focus upon the person asking the questions 90% of the time; 10% glancing at panel members.

The idea behind them is that it allows all interested parties in the role to assess you jointly, but also allows individuals to put collectively assess your evidence often putting different interpretations on it.

Unstructured interviews

These are as it implies, totally unstructured and free flowing, often used by untrained interviewers as the basis of their selection. The free flowing nature makes them better for the candidates, but can result in evidence being gained that is inconsistent across a group of people.

At one extreme the interview could end up being entirely about football. However this is unlikely as the interviewer is still likely to concentrate on the job role.

By preparing answers as if it were a competency based interview, even though unstructured, you can interject with examples that demonstrate your ability.

If you feel that you have not had a chance to really cover all your skills towards the end of the interview, the best way to get across some extra points is at the end when you are asked if you have any questions. By asking leading questions that are carefully phrased you can highlight your relevant experience. For instance if the advert highlights the need for customer service:

'I saw in the advert that you are looking for someone with good customer service skills, I've worked in a customer service role for over 5 years', I was wondering how much customer interaction there will be in the role?' highlighting your 5 years' experience.

Informal interviews

Although asked along for a chat and an informal interview, there is no such thing. It is still an interview whether it is over lunch, dinner, or in a coffee shop. Prepare as if it were a full blown competency based interview.

Going to meet the team for a coffee could have you in a room with 14 people all asking you questions.

Competency based / behavioural based interviews

Many employers now use competency (behavioural) based questions as the basis of their selection interviews.

They use past behaviour as a prediction of future performance, or in simple terms, ask you to provide evidence in the form of you recounting previous experiences and stories, which is then judged and often scored. If the story you recount is strong enough you get good marks, a poor story getting lower marks.

Yes – if the employer is using competency based questions, they score your answers.

Typically you have one person asking the questions, a second writing down everything you say.

This often goes further. As a previously Certified 'Customer Service Assessor', I was asked to recount and write down what I heard, but also asked to record body language and to record what people did during the assessment. They were then scored on both what they said and their body language.

Most interviewers don't have this level of training and so what usually happens after you have left the room, the interviewer and the 'scribe' will review the notes and jointly score you in a number of areas required by the job.

You need to prepare well for such interviews, and although they sound hard, they are really easy *if* you do the preparation in advance.

So let's look at how the questions are derived. To start with an employer will first identify what skills they need a person to have such as to be a team worker, to be able to deliver excellent customer service, or have the ability to cope under pressure. This may include practical skills such as being able to use Excel or Word, but they would be assessed separately.

So the competencies identified might be:

   Must be able to perform effectively as part of a team
   Must be able to effectively organise and prioritise work load

Must be able to deliver excellent customer service

In reality the competencies are often not so straight forward in title, a manager may have competencies including:

Leads Change
Challenges staff to top performance
Drives value creation

So once established, the next step is to develop a set of questions to ask the candidates to allow them to evidence ability in that particular area, such as proving they are a team player. The answers provided may often include more technical evidence, but in the main are situationally based.

For example a Project Manager may be asked to recount the delivery of a project and as part of this interview, the competency required 'to be able to effectively deliver a project'. As part of them describing the project delivery they may go into detail on how they developed a project plan, thus touching on more technical aspects.

In the main the questions start with:

- Can you tell me about a time when...?
- Talk me through a situation when you have...
- Can you give me an example of when...?

In reality competency based questions are very easy to predict – see earlier section on 'Analysing a role'. Once identified, stories can be prepared in advance.

When we say 'stories' these are not made up examples, but examples that need to be well thought through and laid out, having a beginning, a middle, and an end.

Building up answers to competency based questions – STAR technique

So having identified the main skill / experience requirements for the role, you can now start to predict interview questions and prepare answers to those questions.

You also have time on your side to really work on your answers to the skill based questions.

So once you have identified the skill areas (competencies):

1. Take each skill area in turn required by the job role
2. Think of questions the interviewer may ask around this skill area
3. Think of an example to provide to the interviewer to demonstrate you have that skill = you are 'competent' in a particular area
4. Write out the examples / stories and work on them to get them 'spot on'
5. Finally learn the stories

For one skill area there may be several questions that could be asked, and it may mean creating several stories to answer different questions.

The best way to structure your answers is to use either the STAR or IPAR techniques.

STAR is a structure or framework used to help build up stories so that they are well structured and powerful in content.

STAR stands for

> S = Situation – Describe the scene or situation you were in
> T = Tasks – Identify any tasks involved and their importance
> A = Actions – Your actions and what you did to resolve the issues
> R = Results – The benefit / results you achieved

The simple process to build up the stories is to take a blank piece of paper.

- On the top write down the potential question
- Underneath write the work based example you are going to use to demonstrate your ability
- Set it out as follows:

Skill / Question Example	Dealing with a difficult person? Customer complaint last Wednesday
ST	
A	
R	

Just like being at school, use this as a story plan and bullet point key facts under the ST, the A and the R. Some people like to write the whole story out in full, but we suggest bullet points as these can be quicker to learn, tend to provide a good structure, and when recounting the story you can appear more natural because you are not learning the story parrot-fashion.

The ST tend to go together as shown above and it is vital that you set the scene well by explaining in depth if needs be the situation you were in, the problems faced, consequences of something not being done well, and the issues.

© Job Doctor

Too many people do an AR...focusing on their actions and the results without setting the scene properly. Setting the scene is _critical_ for the story to be understood and judged properly.

A simple way of thinking about the content of the story to ensure you cover all areas is to think it is being marked:

> 4 marks for setting the scene = the ST (Situation and Tasks)
> 4 marks for your actions = the A (Actions)
> 2 marks for the measurable and quantifiable result = the R (Result)

When you are preparing the examples for the interview and your stories, some tips are:

- Try and think of work based examples if possible (students are fine to talk about school or college or even social examples)
- Vary your examples for different questions. Repeating the same example time and time again does not show breadth of experience
- Most people work on 4 or 5 stories that can be adapted to a whole range of questioning areas, that should be enough
- If the interviewer knows you, don't assume you don't need to set the scene as well. With competency based interviews your answers are often scored. If a fact is not stated by you, the interviewer is not allowed to fill in the gaps, and only marks what you actually say
- It is what YOU did in the situation and not what WE did. So when recounting the stories don't talk about 'we' when actually you are talking about you, it should be 'I'
- Work on your answers over several days to perfect them
- Don't go into too much depth and technical detail unless relevant. By including it you can often lose the impact of the story
- Stories can be really simple, don't think they have to be long and complicated, they just need to be well structured and show the skills required
- Focus on the actual question when preparing the stories. People tend to try and sell themselves by building in other facts – this can lose the impact of the story. It is vital you keep to the point

As an alternative to STAR the other structure we recommend that is easier for some is IPAR.

> I = Introduction – tell us about the situation
> P = Problem – builds up the issues and problems
> A = Action – what you did
> R = Results – measurable if possible

With both structures try and provide measurable results not just say 'it all worked out well.' How was this identified?

Finally if struggling setting the scene (the ST), look at the end results and what you were trying to achieve. Now turn them into the problem at the start. For example:

Result = Managed to keep the client and grew their business by 10%

Could be turned into:

Situation / Task = Key client was looking to leave, would have lost 100K in sales over the next year. Important to retain them and not lose their business.

STAR video example

Over the years we have looked for videos to really demonstrate how to apply this structure and on YouTube there is a video which we think really demonstrates the STAR structure in action.

Go onto the site and search 'STAR Interview'. Usually the second or third video down is one featuring Jason Jordan – Curtin University (he wears glasses in the picture).

Adapt your stories for different interviews

Remember – although you prepare stories to tell, these may need to change depending upon the application. We recommend that for every job you go through this process, analysing each job role separately and use this information to tweak your stories, or even introduce new examples as required.

Sample competency based questions

For most jobs there are key competencies that crop up time and time again. These tend to be:

Good customer service skills
Team work
Able to organise and prioritise workload
Accurate / High attention to detail
Able to work under pressure
Able to hit set targets and deadlines
Quick to learn / adaptable
Problem solving

Management roles might include:

Ability to motivate and gain the commitment of a team
Ability to deal with underperforming team members
Ability to develop team members
Ability to delegate work effectively
Ability to improve process or operational efficiencies
Ability to work at a strategic level

So what are the questions likely to be? Here are some suggestions:

Customer service skills

- Can you give me an example of where you have delivered exceptional or outstanding customer service?
- Can you tell me about a recent customer complaint or issue you have had to deal with, and talk me through how you effectively resolved it?
- Can you describe to me a difficult person you have dealt with, and talk me through how you won them over?
- Talk me through a situation you have been in where you felt you delivered a high level of customer service
- Give me an example of where you have exceeded customer expectations
- Can you talk me through what you have done recently to improve your customer service skills? (A weaker question but shows self-development)
- Can you give me an example of when you have gone out of your way to help others?
- Can you describe to me the strongest business relationship you have developed and how you built it up?

Team work

- Can you describe the best team you have been part of and why it was such a good team?
- Can you describe your role in your current team?
- Can you give me an example of when you have worked closely with colleagues?

Organisational skills

- Can you give me an example of a situation you have been in where you have had to organise and prioritise your workload?
- Can you describe to me how you organise your workload in your current job?
- Can you give me an example of a typical day in your current role and tell me how you go about organising your workload?

High attention to detail / accuracy

- Can you describe to me a time when you have had to work to high levels of accuracy and tell me why it was so important?

Able to work under pressure

- Can you describe to me a situation when you have had to work under pressure?
- Tell me about a recent event where you felt under pressure

<u>Able to hit set targets and deadlines</u>

- Can you describe to me a situation you were in when you were about to miss a target or deadline, and how you reacted?
- Talk me through what targets and deadlines you currently work to
- Talk me through how you ensure you meet your current targets

<u>Quick to learn / adaptable</u>

- Can you give me an example of a situation you have been in where you have had to change and learn new concepts?
- Can you give me an example of when you have had to get up to speed very quickly?

<u>Problem solving</u>

- Can you describe to me a recent problem you have had, and how you went about resolving it?
- Describe to me the most innovative idea you have come up with to a problem
- Talk me through how you analysed a recent problem, and the solution you came up with

Management:

<u>Ability to motivate and gain the commitment of a team</u>

- Can you give me an example of a team you have taken over, and how you gained their commitment?
- Can you describe to me a team member, and what you do to motivate that individual to top performance?
- Can you talk me through your team, and how you motivate each member to ensure top performance?

<u>Ability to deal with underperforming team members</u>

- Can you describe to me a team member who was underperforming and how you dealt with that situation?
- Can you tell me about an individual in your team who was resistant to change and how you won them over?

<u>Ability to develop team members</u>

- Can you describe to me an individual you have developed to top performance and how you supported them in that journey?

<u>Ability to delegate work effectively</u>

- Can you talk me through how on a daily basis you focus your team and ensure all tasks are completed on time?
- Talk me through how you organise your team's workload?

<u>Ability to introduce process or operational improvements</u>

- Can you give me an example of an improvement you made to a business?
- Talk me through something you have introduced into a business that made an impact

<u>Ability to work at a strategic level</u>

- Can you give me an example of where you have worked at a strategic level?
- Tell me about the last strategic decision you made

As you can see, the questions are not difficult to work out once you have the skill or competency identified.

Some questions above are very similar, and this is not deliberate but a fact. What interviewees don't realise is that there are only so many questions an interviewer can ask and so often the same question is phrased in a different way to try and be more original – but it is still the same question at the end of the day.

<u>More help building up your 'stories'</u>

If you are struggling with thinking up examples to provide in an interview or are not sure your stories are strong enough and want them reviewed by an experienced interviewer, Job Doctor provides Skype and telephone support (purchased by the hour) to UK and International clients.

For details please refer to our website www.job-doctor.com

Portfolio based interviews

Are you in a creative role or working in areas such as architecture, design or web development? Portfolio based interviews are where you are asked to take samples of your work with you, and the interview is around your portfolio.

When choosing work examples to take with you research the company and choose pieces or diagrams that are relevant to the job role and their organisation. You may have favourite pieces that you feel are impressive, but it is not about what you feel is good, it is all about what they want to see.

Strength based interviews (SBI)

Graduate recruiters such as Nestlé and Ernst & Young are now using strength based interviews.

The interviewer focuses upon what you like doing and what you have a natural aptitude for, rather than what you can do. They are trying to get to understand your strengths; the belief is that if you do what you enjoy, you enter a state of consciousness known as 'flow'. Not getting too complicated, this should lead to greater productivity.

Typical questions are:

- What do you enjoy doing in your spare time?
- Tell me about something you are especially proud of
- What tasks do you tend to leave until last on your to-do list?
- What is your biggest weakness?
- When are you happiest?
- When would your friends and family say you are happiest?
- What for you is successful day?
- Describe a situation when you feel most like yourself
- Tell me about a task or activity that you feel you excel at
- Tell me about a task or activity that you do well
- What were your favourite subjects at school?
- What unique qualities could you bring to our organisation?
- What inspires you most?

How do you prepare for them? Prepare answers for the questions above and look at TheStudentRoom.co.uk or WikiJobs.co.uk to see if previous applicants have posted details on other possible questions.

Value based interviews

When an organisation has social, ecological, political or environmental foundations, interviews may focus upon company or business values.

In our opinion such interviews can be the worst to undertake and are hard to predict exact questions for.

They are difficult to handle as they focus on the business values and require a lot of quick thinking. They may also take into account your views on political or other issues impacting upon their business.

Preparation can help.

For instance a teacher may be asked about their view on student testing, a nurse upon current government policies and funding. In both cases their social values may be explored and thus their reasons for following their profession.

More difficult questions are pure value based and often cover areas such as: collaboration; commitment; compassion; diversity; flexibility; innovation; integrity; quality; responsibility; and trust.

Sample value based questions:

Collaboration

- Tell me about a time when you put aside your own needs to help others
- Tell me about a time when you displayed loyalty and commitment to others
- Tell me about a time you disagreed with the course a project or activity was taking
- Tell me about a time others failed to support you and it had a negative impact upon your own activity
- Coping strategies can help high pressurised situations. Describe a time when you have used coping strategies to get a job done
- Describe a time when you had to develop effective working relationships in order to complete a task
- Tell me about a time when you were unclear of what you should be doing and how you reacted

Commitment

- Describe a time when you demonstrated commitment to another individual
- Describe to me a time when you went out of your way to get a job or task completed

Compassion

- Can you tell me about a time when you were perceptive to others' feelings and needs?
- Describe to me a time when a colleague showed you compassion at work
- Work is often stressful and keeping a compassionate and positive attitude is essential, tell me about such a time
- Describe to me a time when you were especially perceptive to a person's feelings

Diversity

- Tell me about a very difficult work situation you have been in
- Tell me a time you felt threatened and describe how you coped
- What is the greatest challenge you have faced when working with others?
- Tell me about a time you had to adapt quickly to a situation you had little control over

- Tell me about a time when you had to deal with a person who didn't like you
- Describe a situation where you felt your work had been judged unfairly
- Describe to me a time when you felt your intentions had been misunderstood

Flexibility

- We look for individuals who are flexible around business needs. Can you describe a situation where you have demonstrated flexibility in a job?
- Can you tell me about a time when you adapted or altered your plans to ensure a task was completed?

Innovation

- Describe a problem you have had and how you used an innovative idea to overcome it
- Describe a crisis situation you have been in and how you effectively resolved the issues
- Give me an example of a unique solution you have come up with to a problem
- Describe a situation when you have had to adapt your activities to enable you to deal with unplanned issues

Integrity

- Give me an example of when you have expressed an unpopular view point
- Describe to me a time when you have spoken up as you felt others were wrong
- Tell me about a time when you failed to follow procedure in order to get a job completed more efficiently
- Describe a situation you were in when you last failed to follow the set procedure and did things your own way

Quality

- Tell me about the last suggestion you made to improve operational efficiencies
- How do you ensure your work achieves the quality required by the business?
- Give me an example of when you made a serious error in your work
- When was the last time you made an error in your work?
- Describe a recent task which you have completed that required high levels of accuracy and quality work

<u>Responsibility</u>

- What was the last mistake you made in your job, and what did you do about it?
- What policies or procedures do you follow in your current job that you think are wrong?
- Describe a time when you have supported a colleague by coaching or mentoring them to help them do a better job
- What jobs or tasks do you leave until last?
- Tell me about a time when you have 'stood up and been counted'

<u>Trust</u>

- Describe to me how you build up trust with others
- Describe to me a time when you put great trust in another person
- What would you do if others felt you untrustworthy?
- Tell me about a time you have helped motivate others
- Tell me about a situation where you identified a problem and dealt with it so it did not grow into a larger issue

For all the above, there are a number of follow on and probing questions an interviewer may then ask.

Some value based questions can combine two values:

We believe in valuing people we support and being flexible around their needs. Can you please describe a situation which demonstrates your own ability to value a person and your own flexibility with regards their needs?

Integrity in how we support people along with an ability to show compassion is important to our business. Can you give me an example which demonstrates your own ability to show compassion and integrity to another person?

We value the rights of children and believe in standing up for them. Can you give me an example of where you have gone out of your way to protect the rights of a child?

To prepare for value based interviews use the STAR structure. Start by looking at the company website as it may provide hints to value based questioning. If there is a mention of the business values, take notes, then try and think of examples that could demonstrate your own values are close to theirs. Refer back to the suggested questions above to help in your preparation.

Value based questions often appear in vocational interviews, so be clear in your motives to become a doctor, nurse, teacher, etc.

Technical interviews

Technical questions are usually in-depth questions about your knowledge, training and expertise. If a software developer, this might include questions about coding or testing methodology. For a solicitor it may include questions about legal precedent or practice.

Often the employer will testing your skills in an area by also asking you to undertake a practical test such as providing you with a sample of code to review and identify problems with (if a software developer).

But for most, technical questions are asked by an interviewer with a good understanding and knowledge of the subject, so you need to know your stuff.

If likely to be asked technical questions our advice is to refresh your memory about your subject area by researching on the internet or pulling out old text books. The job descriptions along with person specifications often highlight areas you might be involved in were you to secure the role. So focus upon refreshing your memory in these subject areas, surfing the internet for information, and be informed on your subject area as best as possible.

Graduates may have left university and not been actively involved in a subject area for several months or even years. So if you are a quantity surveyor graduate applying for trainee quantity surveyor role, it is imperative that you refresh your knowledge on the subject areas prior to your interview.

Research IT systems

Even if not undertaking a technical interview, in job advertisements there is often reference to IT Systems which you may or may not have used. An advert might highlight the company uses 'the SAP accounts package' and further state 'full training will be provided'. So you apply and get the interview. On your CV it does not list SAP as a package you have used and after all you have the interview, so you turn up not having researched it.

Then the question comes 'Have you used the SAP accounts package before?' or harder still 'How much do you know about the SAP accounts package?'

Your answer – 'not used it and I know nothing about it….'

Had you spent even ten minutes on the internet Googling it your answer could be so much better and stronger. In addition you are showing that you are keen on the role having taken time out to research the system.

It would sound better if your answer was 'I've read a few articles about the package and from what I've seen it seems to be very similar to the SAGE Line 50 package I used in my last job, so I think I should be able to pick it up quite quickly'.

So research everything in the advertisement you have not heard of.

Situational / scenario interviews

Another way of assessing the potential of an individual is to ask scenario based questions. This is where the interviewer puts you in a hypothetical situation and asks you how you would react. From the response the interviewer is able to identify potential problem solving skills, customer services skills, reasoning and common sense skills, along with a lot more.

This sounds like a less scientific way of judging a person in theory, but in reality it is replicating elements of Assessment Centres where candidates are put through a series of exercises to actually demonstrate their ability such as role plays.

Organisations such as Marks & Spencer have taken this to a very high level. If you apply on line for a role at M&S you start by answering a range of situational based questions as a pre-screen. You are given several possible answers to choose from. Getting through the written questions you are then further screened by watching short videos where you have to decide what you would do next from several possible options.

A common retail scenario based question is:

'If you have a head office director who needs information urgently for a meeting in 5 minutes, a customer asking for you on the shop floor, and a delivery driver at the back door who needs paperwork signing; who would you deal with first and why?'

The answer:

First – The customer, they always come first
Next – The delivery driver, as if on a timed delivery schedule they could easily give up waiting and not drop off the goods. You are there after all to sell goods in retail
Finally the director – Who would expect you to help the customer first and get the stock into the store to sell

Another common question is:

'You have a large amount of work to complete and working to a tight deadline. Your manager a week before the deadline tells you it has been brought forward by 3 days. What would you do?'

The recruiter is looking for common sense and this might mean: working late; asking for colleagues help; reprioritising; telling your manager that you need help.

Situational questions are mainly used in entry level or volume recruitment situations where employers are trying to identify raw traits or abilities. We have however seen them also used at senior level.

Case study / article interviews

These are used to test your commercial awareness. At the start of your interview you are provided with an article to read, often an obscure news article. You are then asked questions about the article with the interviewer looking at how you process information and answer questions about it. These are hard to prepare for.

Assessment centre interviews

Assessment centres are where several potential candidates are brought together to undertake a number of exercises that may include role play, in-tray, and group exercises. An in-depth guide is available from our website www.job-doctor.com.

In addition there will be either one or two interviews: a technical interview to test subject knowledge; and a competency based interview so prepare as discussed earlier.

As with group interviews, remember to also prepare questions for 'small talk'.

Psychometric testing interview questions

When you are asked to complete a Psychometric Personality Questionnaire the exercises nowadays tend to be completed on-line. Within seconds the results are with the recruiter and as part of the results, questions are generated by the test, questions to be used in an interview to confirm and help validate the profile.

Yes the profiles are not always 'black and white' but often have grey areas, however many companies do use them as screening tools with a pass or fail.

Having completed the test, when you are interviewed, the interviewer may use some of the questions generated by the personality profile to explore further areas of potential concern. Also areas where they need to ensure the results are accurate: the grey areas.

A Psychologist would at this point say all tests are not as good as each other, but if you are about to attend an interview having completed a personality profile, there is a way to prepare for it. Take a personality test by buying one for yourself and seeing how you are viewed by it. On the internet there are various online personality tests that you can purchase off a number of websites in both the UK and abroad.

The results should give you a fair idea of what your profile should say about you, and if you purchase the correct test, it will also generate questions that an interviewer might ask you. You can then prepare answers to potential questions they may ask.

We can't recommend tests, but use one based upon D.I.S.C. as this is the basis for many personality profiles used (Dominance, Influence, Steadiness and Compliance).

Competency based video interviews

A technique which has been used by a number of Recruitment Agencies since the 90s is to include video as part of the interview process. This is not a common technique but worth a mention.

To start with the recruitment consultant will interview and video the recruiting line manager asking them about the role and their expectations, requirements etc. This is then shown to the applicant in the interview to confirm they are still interested in the job, providing a 'realistic job preview'. If still interested, the applicant is then videoed answering a number of competency based questions. This is then shown to the recruiting line manager as part of the pre-screen.

The technique if done properly is very effective allowing line managers to hear evidence from candidates relevant to their roles, and quickly select ideal candidates to progress to the face to face interview.

A number of employers have used this technique to recruit staff including Virgin and I Bank of Scotland. Today we are unsure of who still use the technique.

Second interviews / meeting the team

If you get a second or final interview it is important to remember that the job is not in the bag until you are offered it. Treat all interviews as if they were your first and expect surprises.

If you get an invitation to come in for a few hours and meet the team, this could mean sitting in a room with ten individuals asking a barrage of questions, not the expected friendly walk around the building and quick hello with lots of coffee!

If you are with someone you have not met before this means you are back at the start in reality, needing to impress all over again. So rehearse your answers and refresh your knowledge.

Meeting the managing director

The Managing Director (MD) often wants to see who his managers are proposing as good recruits. Often, only one person will go forward to meet the MD and, as such, confidence in getting the job is high for the candidate. But this is the most difficult of all situations, as you may have to re-sell yourself from scratch within 20 minutes.

Treat these interviews as if they were the first interview and be confident, personable and enthusiastic about the role; prepare thoroughly.

Common interview questions

When we say common interview questions, these are over 150 of the most asked questions. Some are specific to different roles, some seem daft and stupid, but they are all asked in interviews. We have tried not to include competency based questions amongst them as these need to be prepared based upon the job information, although one or two have slipped in.

Some employers mix competency and non-competency based questions together although they are not meant to.

Our advice even if going to a competency based interview is to prepare answers to ALL of those relevant below. You might just be subtly asked these as you are given a tour of the building or mixed in with the competency based ones.

Question variations

Interviewers tend to ask the same question in slightly different ways to try and appear more intelligent or because that is how they phrase a question.

Often they are trying to catch you out by phrasing the question differently.

The main issue with these questions is that most are subjective and not objective. By seeking your thoughts and opinions the interviewer is not objective in their assessment.

But these questions are widely used, and why? Few interviewers undergo formal interview training and these are often questions they were asked in their job interviews in the past, so they use them when interviewing themselves. Also if your CV is written well, they know what skills and experience you offer, so the interviewer may then be more interested in you as a person.

There is often no definitive answer to many of the questions below, but we have tried to give you an idea on strong answers for some, or how you should approach building up your own answers.

If you have used the Mind Mapping technique and identified the key skill requirements for a role, you can include these skills in your answer to good effect.

The top questions

What are your strengths? What would you bring to this role? Or other alternatives: **What can you do for us that someone else cannot? We are considering two other candidates, what makes you better than them? We have other applicants, why should you get the job instead of them? What are you good at? We have seen better candidates, why should we choose you?**

This is the ideal time to really sell your ability and self to an employer and highlight your skills and experience. You could say 'Hard working, reliable and adaptable' but these do not really sell you to an employer as they tend to be standard answers. Try and think of more original traits.

A simple way to strengthen your answer is by highlighting some of the skills required by the role. For example: looking back at the post room example where organisational, people and administration skills were highlighted you could answer by saying:

'I'm well organised, good with people; and I believe I have good administration skills...'

This answer highlights key requirements identified in the job analysis and the interviewer also hears what they are looking for in their ideal recruit. BUT don't be too obvious and rattle off every single skill requirement, maybe add a few more general strengths such as time keeping, hard-working etc. A good answer recently started:

'Rather than tell you what I think. In my last appraisal my old boss highlighted...'

Alternatively when answering this question you could focus upon other personal strengths that might be useful in the role such as tenacity, team work, commitment.

If you are struggling in preparing an answer, ask a colleague or friend, but remember they have only seen you in certain environments and may not really know all your abilities. Or maybe consider undertaking a personality profile which should highlight key strengths.

How would you describe yourself?

Similar to the previous question, but this can be much more personal in nature. Try and steer this down the skill route if possible.

If you had to describe yourself in three words, what would they be? And why?

In reality similar to the strengths question and in actual fact once you have identified these three words they can be the basis of a number of questions. Good words to choose should be relevant to the role, but may have different interpretations:

Friendly = Gets on well with people, good at relationship building
Committed = Gets the job done, target focussed, hard working
Adaptable = Help out others, willing to develop as a person

After you have highlighted the three words, expect to be asked 'Why...?'

Other questions they can be used to answer include: What are your strengths? What skills will you bring to this job? We are interviewing other candidates, why should you get the job and not one of them?

Here are a few suggestions to consider:

Adventurous	Articulate	Adaptable	Ambitious
Analytical	Controlled	Capable	Challenging
Committed	Competitive	Careful	Confident
Conscientious	Consistent	Consultative	Creative
Conventional	Decisive	Determined	Diplomatic
Efficient	Empowering	Entrepreneurial	Enthusiastic
Fair	Flexible	Friendly	Genuine
Generous	Honest	Helpful	Independent
Influential	Innovative	Inspirational	Imaginative
Knowledgeable	Logical	Loyal	Motivational
Methodical	Optimistic	Organised	Original
Obliging	Outgoing	Persistent	Persuasive
Pioneering	Positive	Practical	Pragmatic
Precise	Professional	Proactive	Patient
Perceptive	Perfectionist	Reliable	Resilient
Resourceful	Responsible	Resolute	Realistic
Self-Reliant	Structured	Sincere	Supportive
Systematic	Satisfied	Stimulating	Thoughtful
Tolerant	Unique	Versatile	Visionary

What do you offer us as your potential new employer?

A similar question to what are your strengths? Highlight how your skills match the role and other personal useful traits. If you have identified the skills you can even refer to them and then link this to previous jobs and situations you have been in to show your ability.

What are your weaknesses? What personal traits get in the way of you performing your job? Why should I not give you the job? What are your developmental areas?

A very risky and 'killer' question if you are not careful. There are a number of ways to answer it:

- Please try <u>not</u> to be predictable by saying 'I'm a perfectionist'. People use it because it is often seen as a positive as it implies they make sure the job is done perfectly...but it also implies they may be a slow worker being bogged down with the detail. For some roles such as an accountant or payroll manager it is a good answer as their jobs are detail focused, and if you do use this answer, highlight that 'It sounds a cliché...but...'
- If in a role such as a payroll manager, highlight what some would see as a weakness but for the role is ideal. For example 'I tend to want to know all the facts before I make a decision, so I'm not the quickest decision maker'. On the surface a negative answer, but employers want you to be pedantic and want you to get all the facts before releasing potentially thousands of pounds

- Try to turn the question into a positive. 'My biggest weakness is that I probably work too hard and my personal life takes second place'. What you're actually saying is that you are very committed to a job. But this is a very common answer and in many text books. 'My other half never sees me' is also a cliché so again try not to use these
- Highlight a training need everyone would have this starting a new job. People usually need to learn about new products or systems, but also highlight that 'I'm a quick learner' so the weakness is downplayed. This is possibly the safest and best answer to the question
- Identify a real weakness and then tell the interviewer what you have done to resolve the problem. To really strengthen your answer, provide an example to demonstrate your technique in action. This is not actually answering the question as it is not 'What used to be your weaknesses'. But most people get away with answering this way
- Turn this into a selling opportunity. 'For the role in question I don't think I have any weaknesses, because...' You must tell them why by matching yourself to the job. Be careful not to sound arrogant and notice the focus is upon the job role, never simply say you have no weaknesses – everyone has some
- Identify something that does not impact upon the job. 'My hand writing is not the easiest to read, but I use a computer these days'
- A common answer is 'chocolate'. If you are going to use this one, be prepared for an experienced interviewer to push for more relevant examples

Students and younger people have an easy answer (providing they have not worked for any length of time). 'Having not held a job before I'm not really sure yet what my weaknesses at work are'

IMPORTANT – Prepare this answer well and reflect on your answer. Does your chosen weakness impact on your ability to do the job applied for? What is the most negative interpretation? Could your answer lose you the job?

You MUST have an answer to this question, it is a very common question and without an answer you create a bad impression

---

Tell me about yourself?

This is a hated question as what do you focus upon? Very common as an opening question and without preparation what do you say?

To start you might ask them what they would like to know about you, but this seldom helps you as the interviewer probably doesn't know themselves. 'A bit about you' can be the unhelpful reply.

So let's go back to the post room and the skills required by the role – Good people skills, well organised. A simple answer is to talk through your CV in a more general way.

'I left school at 18 and since then I've been working in a number of administration roles. I initially worked for a finance company but was in an office on my own and I've always liked helping and being around people, so I moved to JBS. I served customers on the counters and I really enjoyed that job as I got to meet new people daily and built up good relationships with some of the main clients.' And so on...

You can be personal in your answer, married with a son of... or even talk about your hobbies. To gain most impact though keep your answer work related and if you have prepared well for a CV interview, use this preparation as a means to answer this question.

What sort of a person are you?

Referring to the skills needed by the role, use them to help focus your answer. Your answer can be similar to 'What are your strengths?'

Career questions

Where do you see yourself in 2, 3 or 5 years' time?

They want to know how ambitious or un-ambitious you are. Yes, un-ambitious also. If the role has no promotion prospects, by saying you are ambitious may lose you the job; and vice versa. Also are you applying for the role on the table or their boss? It might be that you will be in the job for 5 or 6 years before progression is even thought about, especially if applying for a graduate entry role.

You need to fully understand the opportunities in the company to answer this question well.

It may be best to 'sit on the fence' in your answer 'I can see this as being a role I would enjoy and so could still be in it in a few years' time, however, I'm also one to take opportunities as they come along'. Then ask the interviewer what opportunities do exist.

Where do you see your career going in the future?

Similar to the question above – be realistic and maybe 'sit on the fence' if not sure of the opportunities with this employer.

Why did you choose this career path?

They want to know where you are coming from, what motivates you, try to avoid 'Oh I seemed to fall into...' and talk about aspects you enjoy.

Looking back, what would you have done differently in your career?

This assumes you may have made a career blunder. In reality it is fine to say 'nothing', and if probed talk about all the positive aspects of your career.

Moving to X was a bad move wasn't it? You should have stayed at Y

A more challenging interviewer may put you on the spot and phrase the question in a more direct manner. If you have prepared for a CV interview as part of your general preparation you should be able to justify the move in a more positive light.

How successful do you think you have been in your career so far?

Certainly do not say you are a failure! Try to focus upon your achievements, and link together career moves and actions to show a planned set of career moves.

What would you be looking to achieve in the first 3 or 6 months? How long would it take before you made a meaningful contribution to our organisation?

The most likely reason you are asked this question is because the company needs you to be up to speed and contributing to their organisation very quickly. Your answer should reflect this, but also be realistic.

Do you prefer to work for a large organisation, or a small company? Why?

Your research should give you an idea of their company size so try to relate your answer to them. You may want to sit on the fence. 'Either. I think a small organisation offers greater responsibilities, a larger one more opportunities.' If you have worked for both you might at this stage highlight the fact.

You have not been with your current employer a long time, why are you looking to move now?

The answer could be 'broken promises' but you need to be careful how you phrase things. Ask yourself why you are looking for a new job and be as honest as possible.

It is OK to state the role was only a stop gap in some instances such as a graduate who took a low level role after graduating and whilst looking for a career start. But generally be careful if highlighting this as it may go against you with some employers.

You have been with your current employer a long time, why are you only now looking to move?

New opportunity, time to move on, career blockage, are all reasonable answers. Ask yourself why you are looking for a new job and be as honest as possible.

You have changed jobs a lot. Why was that? You have had a lot of jobs, how do I know you are going to stay if we offer you the job?

A key part of preparing for an interview is working out why you are likely to be rejected. If you have had a number of previous job roles you should have prepared a set answer to get around this. You have made it to the interview, so it could not have been such a negative thing for the recruiter.

If you have analysed the role as described previously, to now highlight parts of the job role and how they are exactly what you love doing can work well here. It shows real thought and consideration have gone into your application.

Another technique is to highlight that you are aware you have moved frequently in the past trying to justify the moves, but are now looking for an opportunity to settle down into a long term role.

If previous roles have been part time or contract / temporary jobs, this task is made easier if you highlight the fact on your CV also. By doing so they may not even ask the question, accepting their temporary nature.

Personal questions

How do you take criticism? What was the last time your boss told you off? And how did you react?

No one takes it well, but a boss wants to feel you will listen to it and take on-board their ideas, certainly not bear a grudge for a few weeks. The fact you are asked this question may imply the interviewer has had staff who took criticism badly. Simple answer is to say 'If constructive I take criticism well. No one is perfect'.

How do you handle conflict? Can you describe a time when you stood up for someone else?

The role you are applying for may place you in a situation where conflict can occur or there could be a difficult colleague you don't know about yet. A good answer is to provide an example to demonstrate how you have dealt with a real life situation in the past based upon STAR.

What makes you angry?

Everyone has something that 'flicks the switch'. Maybe highlighting all the things might not be beneficial here as you don't want to appear to be a hot head. Try and think of something small or even not relevant. 'When driving I hate people who fail to indicate when moving across carriageways' or 'People who drop litter' which also might highlight your social responsibility.

How do you like to be managed?

To answer this question well, you need to understand the individual you will be working for. If their preferred management style is to have daily reports or conversations, to state that you like to be left alone to get on with things may not go down too well, or vice versa.

A way of dealing with this is to turn the question back on them and state that you are quite open to different management styles. Ask them how they would want to manage you. Interviews are two way processes and by asking this question you can identify if their style is one you can work under and reflect on whether this is the job for you.

Alternatively you could state you are happy to be left alone or monitored closely, then providing examples of where you have worked under both regimes.

Who has been your best manager, and why?

They are trying to identify how you like to be managed again. They will make direct comparisons with their own style. Sitting on the fence and providing two examples that demonstrate different styles may be best.

Would you describe yourself as being creative or innovative? Why?

Not everyone is creative and it may be enough to say 'Personally, no. But I know how to learn from others and I try to apply and ensure best practice.'

If you are creative they will often ask for an example.

Look at the role and think about the job, does it need creativity? Or does the advert imply the need to make changes? Although you are not creative you may be asked for examples of where you have improved business models which includes introducing new ideas. So try and think of examples in advance of the interview.

What is the most innovative or creative idea you have come up with? What was the last good idea you came up with?

Think of something you have done to maybe improve a situation. It doesn't have to be a massive or major idea. The recruiter is seeing if you think around issues and look at solutions to solve them.

Describe to me the last problem you had to deal with?

Similar question to the last, but they are looking at how you resolve issues. Think of a STAR based example.

How would you describe your personality?

Jolly; miserable; overpowering; depressing; easy going; laid back. This can be turned into an opportunity to talk about your strengths, but be careful: Laid back can imply lazy; easy going says you are a push over and implies a weak manager.

An interviewer taking on a more challenging interview style may throw these comments back at you with negative connotations.

How would your boss describe you? How would your colleagues describe you?

This is a good chance to sell yourself with terms such as hard working, self-motivated, dedicated etc. Honesty may not be the best policy when answering in some instances particularly if you don't get on together well. What they are actually often asking is 'how would you describe yourself?'

If you have analysed the key skills involved in the role this is a perfect time to highlight them as your own.

How do you feel about carrying out mundane or repetitive work?

'No problem' if the role includes such tasks. Try to give an example of where you have previously carried out similar mundane tasks.

Which parts of your current role do you dislike or find boring?

The interviewer will make direct comparisons to the job on offer. If you state you dislike a key part of the role, you will be shooting yourself in the foot.

Describe your ideal job to me?

A risky question, as you may outline a number of traits that are not in the job you are applying for. Best to describe in a roundabout way the job on offer or even say 'This one because...'

How would you define success?

Try not to focus on money, a big house, or a Ferrari. You could talk about achieving short term goals, bringing up your children to be happy and responsible citizens. Possibly focus upon a personal achievement or your career successes. Or to be happy in a job that is making a difference to people's lives (if in such a role)

What parts of our job do you think you would not enjoy?

Simple answer is 'None'. Highlight any aspects and you are shooting yourself in the foot. You may want to highlight what appeals to you about the job.

What motivates you? What gets you out of bed in the morning?

Money is not always a good answer: Challenge; Opportunity; Enjoyment? Although for some sales jobs the answer may be 'money and the satisfaction of winning a new account'.

What attracts you to this role?

Why did you apply in the first instance? To merely state 'because it is a job that pays money' will not go down well. Highlight elements of the job that appeal, or how it builds on previous experience. You can include aspects such as your long term career goals.

Be careful if highlighting training as this can imply inexperience unless you are new to the job market or looking for a career change.

If you have taken time to break down the role into skill areas you can now start to highlight aspects of the job to good effect and link these to your previous experience.

If we look back over the last year, have you changed at all or learnt any new skills? How have you developed personally in the last year?

The answer may be 'nothing' due to being an experienced individual, but if stating this you might be sounding arrogant. So try and identify something as employers often look for ongoing self-development. 'Nothing' is not a good answer.

How do you keep your skills up to date?

A similar question to that above, the interviewer is looking to see whether you seek self-development and the tools and methods you use.

What is your personal development plan for the next year?

Have you even got one? Employers often encourage self-development and want you to be looking to improve. You might talk about looking to keep your industry knowledge up to date, improve your IT Skills; but be careful not to highlight these in a way that could go against you with regards suitability for the role.

What are your core values?

Aimed more at roles in the third / charity sector possibly, employers may want to see you have integrity in what you do. Answers around: honesty; reliability; dedication; and commitment can all go down well. You might want to refer back to the table of words earlier in this guide for ideas.

Also think about core values for the role. If dealing with money 'honesty' would be key value and should be included in you answer.

What do people think about you that is wrong?

They are trying to identify a personal trait that is taken the wrong way, or even a real trait that you know is wrong.

There is no real right answer for this question. People highlight that when in a group situation they can be quiet, or that people think they are slow decision makers.

With both the trick is to say 'however...' and justify your quietness. 'I like to assess a situation and people before opening up'. Or 'People think I'm a slow decision maker but in reality I like to get all the facts first before deciding'.

What gets you stressed at work? How do you respond under stress?

© Job Doctor

The ideal answer is 'nothing' gets you stressed, but will the interviewer accept this? Most jobs will put you in a stressful situation, so it may be better to highlight a time when you were under stress, and then talk about how you deal with it. You could mention as part of your answer how you enjoy working to deadlines and targets.

How do you cope with pressure?

This implies there is pressure in the job role. 'Well' is the obvious answer and by providing an example of when you have been in a pressurised role or situation will add depth to your answer. However you might not like pressurised roles and you may want to ask them about the expected pressure to help you decide if the role is right for you.

What business culture do you work best in? How would you describe the culture of your current company?

They are looking at whether you will fit into their culture. If you have worked for different types of cultures highlight the fact rather than focus upon one. You may not have ever thought about your employer's culture before, now might be a good time to do so as you may work better in some cultures than others.

Remember to ask how they would describe their culture as well. It is a two way process and this fact might put you off their organisation.

What is your preferred style of working?

Similar question to 'do you like to work on your own or as part of a team?' but combined with 'how do you like to be managed?' and 'what business culture do you work best in?'

Take elements from all these areas in your answer.

What is the last big decision you have had to make?

Are you able to make decisions or do you only ever follow? Even if not a major decision you need an example to give, possibly use STAR.

Relationship questions

How good are you at building relationships? Tell me about the most successful / strongest business relationship you have developed?

It could be with a supplier, customer or colleague in another part of the business. The best way is to provide a STAR based example.

How do you deal with difficult people? Who is the most difficult person you have had to deal with / win over, and how did you get them on your side? Give

me an example of a difficult client / colleague relationship you have been able to win round?

What they want to see is how you can get people round to your way of thinking and win them over, and how you approached the situation. These are competency based and more likely to be asked than the general first question.

Sales questions

What has been the most difficult sale? Who has been the most difficult client you have been able to gain business from and how did you win them over?

This does not have to be a large sale, just an example of a difficult individual who you 'won over' and gained business from.

Which sale are you most proud of and why?

Try and give a different example to the previous question. Talk maybe of the complexity or difficulty.

What do you need to earn to make you comfortable?

Often asked in sales or performance targeted role where bonuses, based on performance, are paid. An employer is looking for you to still be hungry for more money and success, even if you are on a £250k basic salary.

How do you handle rejection?

Again try to give an example. This question is commonly used for junior sales related roles. Do not say 'badly.' Read between the lines, if things are not going well for you, can you pick yourself up, put it behind you, and move on.

Sell me this pen?

A very old question still used by employers. Focus upon 'Needs Features Benefit' statements.

> **BE WARNED** – An old technique still used by interviewers with sales people is to interject loudly words such as 'chemistry', 'rhubarb' or 'thunder' during the interview to see if they can carry on the conversation and pick up the thread.

Motivation to change jobs questions

Why do you apply for this job? Why do you want this job? What attracts you to this role?

Highlight aspects that appeal to you and possibly reference to the company.

How did you hear about this job?

A straight forward enough question with the recruiter sometimes wanting to see if it was by personal referral or you had been following the company's job board.

Do you know anyone who works here?

Be sure whoever you mention will be approached to see what they think about you. Not so good if the person can't stand you!

Can you describe your understanding of what the role involves to me please? What is your understanding of the main challenges in the role? What particularly appeals to you about it?

Make sure you have refreshed yourself on what the advertisement or job description said. In around about way they are seeing if you have understood the purpose and requirements of the role. Being able to recount parts of the advertisement and your interpretation of it demonstrates your interest in the job.

Why are you looking to leave your current job?

Do not criticise your existing employers even if they are dreadful. Safe answers include. 'It is time for me to move on because…', 'I am looking for a new challenge', 'I am looking to progress my career and the opportunities do not exist where I am'.

Do not say you are bored as this projects a negative image.

Why did you leave your last job?

The interviewer may be looking at your motivation and reasons behind your move. They may be digging for any problems you had with your last employer.

If made redundant as part of a general downsizing state that you were one of….made redundant, thus highlighting it was not just you! Or this can be misinterpreted.

Also if you had to re-apply for your job but were not successful, if you do reference this within your answer this may place you in a negative light.

If it was because of a horrible manager, try not to focus upon all your problems as this can make you sound bitter towards your former employer.

Why did you leave your last job? – Compromise Agreements

Now you may have left your last company through an exit or compromise agreement. These are documents that are legally binding and often stop you saying bad things about your old employer and them about you.

In these circumstances you are not able to be honest about the exact situation due to the legal agreement. Thus you need to carefully practice your answer to this question.

Also when recounting the answer you need to focus upon your body language. Often the person is only telling a half story or even a lie when answering this question, so you must make sure your body language doesn't give you away.

What are you looking for in a job? What are you looking for in your next job?

Try and talk about things that relate to the job you are applying for as the interviewer will be making comparisons to the job you have applied for.

Is your current employer likely to make a counter offer if you were to resign? What would you do if your employer made you a counter offer?

Here if you are resolute in your decision to move jobs you need to get this point across. Highlighting it is not just the money as a starting point, but what are you now going to say about why you are looking to change jobs? You need to be clear in why you are looking to leave your current role, if not you will come unstuck at this point.

How long have you been looking for a new job?

There is nothing wrong with saying you have just started, nor is there anything wrong with saying several months, but in the latter case possibly highlight that you are very selective in what you are applying for. If probed to say you have attended twenty interviews and not been offered one job does not sound good, so try and be a little vague about the number of interviews you have attended.

Lots of interviews can also imply you are now well trained in interview technique, so how genuine are your answers?

Housekeeping questions

What is your current salary and what salary are you expecting? What salary are you looking for?

Remember to talk about your whole package not just the basic salary. But be realistic as you could very easily price yourself out of a job.

You may also have been paid a higher salary in your previous role and you will now need to convince the interviewer your reasons for a salary drop or they may see you using them as a stop gap. A simple technique is to highlight that your ex-employer over paid against market rates and that their salary is more realistic. Rehearse this answer very well.

Why are you looking to relocate? How does your family view the possibility of relocation?

This is always a major concern to a recruiter when hiring from out of the area. If possible, evidence a previous relocation experience. Also identify to the interviewer any ties to the area, or a lack of ties elsewhere.

Are you willing to travel as part of the job role?

This often infers overnight stays and if in previous jobs this was required refer back to them. Or simple answer is 'No problem I'm quite happy to travel and stay away as required'. But be honest to yourself 'Happy to stay away one night per week' etc.

How much training do you think you will need to be able to perform this job to the best of your ability?

Another risky question! If you highlight too many areas you are shooting yourself in the foot. Product training and systems training are reasonably safe answers.

Have you taken time off to come here today?' Where does your employer think you are at present?

In other words 'Are you skiving?' Phoney doctors appointment = lying to your current employer. It is best to say that you have taken holiday time off.

What other interviews have you had? What other jobs are you applying for?

Two possible reasons for this question: to see if you are keen to find work similar to the job they have on offer or are applying for anything you see advertised; or they may be trying to see whether they have competition for your services from other employers.

You can mention other jobs, but add the comment 'however, of all the roles, I must say your job seems to be the one I would favour'. Remember an interviewer wants to feel special and that their job is your number one. A common follow on question is:

Looking at the three jobs you have on the go at present, which would be your first choice of jobs if offered all three?'

Unless you say theirs you have just lost any hope of getting the job! Who likes being second best? Over the years so many candidates have said 'well the job next week has better prospects and a better salary' and I sit there wondering 'did you really just say I'm second best?' Interview over and goodbye!

What will your references say about you?

Employers nowadays rarely put anything in a reference other than: Your Name; Job Title; and Dates of Employment. What you actually say here will probably never appear in your reference anyway.

A good answer is to try and highlight some of the job skills of the role applied for but try not to overdo things.

When can you start? How much notice are you on?

A good sign, but not necessarily a job offer. If you are tied into three months' notice, you may want to highlight how you think it might be reduced to a month even if not sure. If the job is vacant, the deciding factor may be how quickly you or another applicant could start. Better to get the job offer and then try to get your notice reduced as most employers are flexible.

If offered the job, how long do you think it will be before you look to move on? How long do you see yourself staying with your next employer?

Although people tend to move jobs every few years, employers still expect employees to make much longer commitments. If you have had a number of very short term roles, the interviewer may need reassurance that you intend to stay.

Have you ever been dismissed or fired from a job?

A very direct question that can put you on the spot! Many people leave jobs under difficult circumstances, change in boss and your face no longer fits, and off you go via a compromise agreement – you did nothing except be a loyal employee for twelve years.

If you have left in a cloud, you need to not only think of your answer but watch your body language as you answer. The interviewer probably knows the tell-tale signs to say you are lying.

So what questions do you have for us?

A question asked at the end of an interview. We suggest preparing a list, writing the questions down and not relying upon your memory. See later section.

Team work questions

Do you regard yourself as working as part of a team currently? What team do you see yourself as belonging to?

If the role you are applying for involves team work, an interviewer may focus upon exiting team work to prove you are a team player.

What types of people do you find difficult to work with?

A risky question unless you fully understand the situation and the people you would be working with. Simple answer is 'none as I get on with most people'.

Do you prefer to work on your own or as part of a team?

Is it a team role? Or stand alone? If not sure sit on the fence and say that you enjoy team work but are sufficiently self-motivated to work on your own. Maybe reference this to an example of where you have been part of a team, but worked independently also.

How would you describe your role in a team? And what do you contribute to team activities?

Think carefully about how you answer this question. You can describe yourself as a leader (if applying for a leader role) or as an idea's person, or an organiser, a person people come to for help.

Are you a team player? Give me an example

The best example is a work related situation, but if you play a lot of sports, team games are also good examples.

What is the best team you have worked in and why?

Describe a situation and why it was a particularly good team to be part of. STAR based example.

Tell me when you have worked as part of a team

Think STAR again, a competency based question but one people tend to generalise about, waffle about. Best have a clear example to impress the interviewer.

> For managers it is important to recognise that they are a team player when sat within their peer group, but when managing their own staff, they are not true team players. They are the boss, telling others what to do.

Management questions

How would you motivate a team and gain their commitment?

If possible provide a real life example to demonstrate your methodology, STAR based.

Tell me about your management style? How would your staff describe you as a manager?

The usual predictable 'firm but fair' often come out here or the newer 'hard but fair', both are cliché answers so be more original.

An original answer would be to talk about being 'collaborative in approach' or 'hands on manager who likes to lead by example' (if that is your style). 'A supportive manager who likes to develop their staff' or maybe 'a strong and decisive leader'

By expanding without being prompted as to why you described yourself that way you are giving evidence to support your claim.

Remember that managers are there to achieve results so you need to provide balanced answers. If you state your style is 'laid back and easy going' this can be interpreted as you 'running a holiday camp'. Balance this answer to include achievement focus 'but staff know what is expected and not to take advantage'.

Managers will also alter their management style to different employees. An experienced employee is often monitored while a new recruit is closely managed. So you might want to highlight altering your style depending upon the individual you are managing, supporting this with examples.

How would you deal with a team member who is not performing? Tell me about a time when you supported a team member who was struggling?

You need to demonstrate both compassion and that you are also willing to take on the responsibility to deal with the situation. Be prepared to mention disciplinary procedures as in any management role you can only tolerate under performance for a short period. A good answer would be to evidence a situation you have been in and how you dealt with it.

The second question may be asked by an employer who takes a more supportive stance on under performance, so try to demonstrate coaching and listening skills.

How do you feel about firing staff?

This is possibly asked because the business needs restructuring or has people issues. You can focus on how you try and correct under performance and see discipline as the last resort. But you may need to take a harder line if the business has serious people performance issues – it may help to ask the background to the question. Most employers want to see a supportive manager, but at the same time don't project yourself as being a soft touch.

How much of your role was 'strategically' as opposed to 'operationally' focused? And can you give me an example of a strategic change you introduced?

A lot of managers think they are strategic but are really operational. The question is very much focused on 'prove you are strategic'. Provide an example of a strategic decision you made and not one you implemented (which is operational).

Would your staff say you are a good manager?

The obvious answer is 'Yes'. The next question will be 'Why?' so you will need to be able to expand upon your answer providing reasons and examples.

What management decisions do you find it difficult to make?

A dangerous question as your answer could demonstrate personal weakness.

What is it that makes you a good manager?

Again, it is asking about your style of management, but you can draw on your experience and exposure to situations.

Looking at your decision making, would you describe your approach as more collaborative or directive? And if you had to put percentages against each, what would they be?

Some people are more directive; others collaborative. This question is similar to 'Describe your management style' but focuses upon decision making in particular.

There is no right and wrong answer, but the interviewer may be looking for an individual who favours one style more than the other. Follow on questions will try and get you to provide examples of your decision making in action.

When managing staff, do you alter your approach or adapt your style of management ever?

Some managers will say they do not alter their style, but in reality a 'dream' employee will be managed differently for an incompetent one. It is also important to provide a balanced answer to show the softer and stronger manager.

What sorts of tasks would you delegate to others?

Try and think of a few examples and the reasons behind your actions.

How do you decide what targets to set for yourself and others?

A management question with the interviewer looking at the reasoning behind target setting. Mentioning stretch targets often gains extra brownie points.

Out of the box thinking questions

If we offered you this job, what is the first thing you would do? How would you approach this job?

To be able to answer this question you need to have a good grasp of the role. If asked this question the interviewer is possibly looking for an action orientated answer and not 'I'd learn where everyone sits…'

On reflection, what would you do differently with your life or in your career to date?

Be careful as it is a risky question. The best answer is 'Nothing'. If it is clear from your CV you have made mistakes possibly admit them if confronted.

What is the most innovative idea you have come up with?

Think of a good example and be prepared to say why it was so good

Looking at your current role, what problems have you identified that had previously been overlooked? What changes did you put into place in your last role? If you had the opportunity, what changes would you introduce in your current business?

If you identified some changes, talk about them. The natural follow on is to be asked 'What did you do about changing things or introducing them?' If you say 'Not a lot', having identified things, the impression is not good. However, if you raised them but were blocked in making changes, it shows how you are looking to add value and improvements to a business, even if you could do nothing with your ideas.

If you had to invite 10 people to a dinner party, anyone you like, who would you invite and why? If you had to be stuck in a lift with five people, who would they be?

A question that reveals more about you than you would think. It can bring out family values, political preferences, highlight your intellectual ability.

If you were an animal, what sort of animal would you be? Why?

A lion, as they are big and strong; a sheep, as I am a follower and do not lead. Some animals are better examples than others. A firm safe bet is a dolphin: team player, family orientated, intelligent, friendly, picks up things quickly.

Name three people you really admire. Why do you admire them?

The answer can show how well read you are, and your personal values. The interviewer may just ask for one person, but think of three to be safe.

What was the last book you read / film you saw? What newspaper do you read?

If you say 'War and Peace' one image of you is projected, 'Harry Potter' a different image, 'The Dangerous Book for Boys' yet another. Remember the interviewer may have also read the book/seen the film and quiz you about it.

As for newspapers, is it The Times, or Daily Star?

What is your claim to fame?

Designed to put you on the spot and test your mental agility. A question often included in assessment centres or group interviews, when you are asked to introduce yourself to the group.

What colour is your brain and why?

Colour psychology and 'grey and mushy' is not acceptable.

Do you have a role model? If so, who and why?

This could either be a family member or a great statesman, sports star. You need to be able to justify why in particular they are a role model for you.

Rank these in order of importance – power; wealth; status; health?

Another version is: challenge; location; advancement; money; security. These questions focus upon your personal priorities with no right or wrong answer; although advancement being first could lose you the job if it has little promotional prospects.

What question should I have asked you as part of the interview that I have not?

A question that can elicit very interesting questions! You could highlight that they have not asked you about one of your skill areas relevant to the job. A safe answer is to say 'I think you have covered everything'. Maybe you could be a little cheeky and say 'you have not asked me if I'd like the job…!'

What lies are on your CV? What is the biggest exaggeration on your CV?

A question designed to put you on the spot, your body language being monitored as you answer possibly. Best to try and bluff this one out if you have stretched the truth. A simple answer is 'none that I'm aware of'.

Tell me about something not on your CV?

A very open question, possibly highlight a keen hobby or interest or even a recent personal achievement that is un-work related. Careful in what you choose though.

Retail questions

If you had three people to deal with: a customer; a delivery; a senior director; who would you deal with first / second / then last?

Common question – customer ALWAYS comes first; delivery if not signed for may mean the driver just drives off without leaving the goods; director last…!

This is a situational or scenario based question. To get some practice with them think about applying to Marks & Spencer on-line as their application process puts you in various scenarios. I'm sure they will not like me suggesting that as a way of honing your skills, but they are a good employer and worth applying to anyway.

Performance questions

What would you say is your greatest achievement to date?

This might not always be your work achievement. 'Bringing up my son / daughter to be a responsible human being' is just as acceptable.

It should ideally be a work related achievement already on your CV.

What has been your biggest success at work?

Your achievements should be included on your CV. Often the interviewer is looking for strong commitment, initiative, innovation and ideas.

What sort of targets have you worked to in the past? And did you achieve those targets?

Be prepared to quote numeric or activity level targets. If you have not had any formal targets highlight working under pressure and achieving deadlines.

How do you decide what targets to set for yourself?

Similar to the management question mentioned earlier, but used this time trying to understand what targets you set yourself. Mentioning stretch targets often gains extra brownie points.

Can you work under pressure and deal with deadlines? What deadlines are you used to working to?

The interviewer wants to hear that you can work under pressure and the best way to demonstrate this is to provide examples based on STAR.

If you get to the end of the day and there are jobs still to be done, how would you deal with this situation?

'Stay late to finish urgent jobs' demonstrates commitment and responsibility.

What decisions do you find it difficult to make?

Already covered under management questions, this is the more general version. Try not to think of something that could highlight personal weakness.

You seem to be a little overqualified for this role; will it really keep you motivated?

The kiss of death for a lot of people, or is it? What they are often doing is testing the water to see how you react. The devious Interviewer may re-phrase the question as 'Looking at your background, would you not see yourself more as a...' Simply disagree with them, but it may be worth first finding out what they are focusing on, 'Why do you think that?'

Talk about how you see the role as interesting, having its own challenges, the fact, possibly that you no longer want to be in a more demanding role, but be careful with this last one. Look them straight in the eye as you answer if you can, as this will convey conviction.

When did you last fail in a task? And what was it?

Be careful what you choose. It may show weakness. To say you never fail may not be accepted. One trick is to lay blame at someone else's door…

Tell me about when you last missed a deadline?

Everyone at some time will miss a deadline. An easy deflection is to blame lack of input from others but stress 'I did all I could to try and hit the deadline.' If you state you have never missed a deadline, expect to be challenged.

From what you know of the role, what do you see as the most important Key Performance Indicators (KPIs)? What KPIs would you set for your staff?

This question is often asked in a watered down way 'What do you think we are expecting from the person who gets the job?' If you have analysed the role properly you should have an understanding of the key elements and potentially expectations, thus suggest potential KPIs.

How do your organise your workload? How do you prioritise your workload?

The interviewer is looking for an answer which includes prioritising, possibly delegating items to others, but above all having a structured approach.

What is the last big decision you have made? Talk me through the last decision you made? When was the last time you used your initiative?

All are looking for you to take ownership of a problem and get a resolution. In these cases think of a STAR based answer if possible.

Give me an example to demonstrate your resilience at work

This is a question asking you to highlight a personal trait, the ability to keep going. So think of an example to demonstrate your resilience.

General / background questions

What do you know about our company?

This is covered in your preparation. We would reiterate our previous advice, to take print outs from their website and produce them now which often impresses.

What do you know about our industry?

This should really be looked at in your research. If they sell hydraulic valves, find out what they are used for. For roles involving selling you will need to identify who their competitors may be, who they sell to, and identify target industries.

Why do you want to work for our company?

A fantastic opportunity to 'sell' yourself, but you must be relevant; good company, exciting job on offer; wonderful opportunity to develop. Unless a graduate or entry level role, do not highlight the training and experience too strongly as this may imply you are in need of a lot of development.

Also – remember an interviewer wants to know that it is the role for you more than the right company, so if you rave about the organisation, rave also about the job on offer.

What hobbies or interests do you have away from work? How do you spend your free time?

Remember that if you state on your CV that you are a keen squash player, they will be expecting this to be included. If you have not played squash for ten years it may be worth removing it from your CV.

Tell me about your family?

An employer may be quite innocently asking it to find out more about you and could be looking for a strong family ethos in new employees. Certain cultures place great store on family values. Family businesses may also look at your values to see how they align with their own values.

HOWEVER – This question can be loaded. Women often get asked this as a way of finding out if they are looking to start a family, or have child care arrangements in place.

Who has been the most difficult person you have worked with?

The interviewer is trying to identify how you deal with conflict. Always refer to an example, but choose it well. If in a management situation, you may provide an example of a staff member who was a problem. It could be a client or work colleague, even your former manager. They are looking for a positive outcome.

How do you maintain a good work / life balance?

Not often asked, this question implies the employer wants you to get the most out of work and home life. It may also be used to identify commitment or lack of it.

Follow on questions may help them identify more about your personal situation and background. Also work habits and how you go about organising your daily work.

Students specific questions

Why did you study…at….?

Employers are often interested in your College / University choice. Try to avoid 'I did not get into the University I wanted to and ended up in clearing'. Why did you choose X? Best course, good reputation, why?

I see you studied (e.g.) Chemistry at University. Do you not want to pursue a career in science?

It may be asked to see if you had a different career in mind. There is no problem stating that you studied a subject purely for interest. Don't answer as one person once did 'there aren't any jobs as chemists at present so I thought I'd do this instead' implying second best and little commitment.

Do your grades reflect your true potential?

Asked maybe to average graded students. You might highlight that you are better with practical exercises and course work, applying your skills rather than sitting exams.

Closing question

Why should we offer you this job?

Often the closing question asked. A perfect time to sell yourself against the job

Highlight the key elements of the role and how you match them. Another is to impress the Interviewer with what you can add to their company, even highlighting extra skills and experience you bring (if you have analysed the job in great detail).

You can also talk about commitment, energy and drive.

> **Remember** – Review prepared answers for each interview, do they need changing for greater impact?

Questions an interviewer should not ask you

Nowadays, legislation prevents interviewers asking questions in several subject areas. Asking such questions could result in criminal proceedings against the interviewer. These areas are:

Sex	Race	Nationality	Disability	Age

If you are ever asked such questions there are several ways of dealing with them:

- Politely state that you feel the question is one you would prefer not to answer, as you do not see it as being relevant to your application.
- Respond as you would anyway and answer the question. An easy way of dealing with many of the inappropriate questions but nevertheless not right.
- Ask a question back such as 'If I was planning to start a family would it have any bearing on my application?'
- Point out that, under legislation, the Interviewer has no right to ask that type of question.
- Ask a very direct question back highlighting the area they are discriminating on 'I think what you were really asking me was whether I could potentially be taking time off in the near future for maternity leave. Is that correct?'
- Ignore the question and re-direct the conversation.

One thing to consider, regardless of your response, your answer could easily cost you the job. But do you want to work for an individual with such values? Be prepared for these tricky and illegal questions.

Men often think they would not be discriminated against due to having children. But if they are not the main bread winner and this fact is revealed, an interviewer looking to discriminate may assume that they take time off if the children are ill.

We would not condone lying, but one approach when asked one of these questions is to volunteer additional information which may not always be accurate. For example 'do you have a family?' which could be asked innocently. Answer 'yes, two children aged 4 and 7. The nice thing is that we have good child care arrangements in place to look after them if they are on holiday or ill'. Whether child care arrangements are in place or not who would know.

'How old are you?' Totally illegal question! Answer 'I'm 63, but financial considerations mean I'm not looking to retire until I'm at least 70', the last part possibly not being true…but identifying you could be with them 7 and not 3 years.

Prepare answers to questions about things you lack

A key part of interview preparation is spotting why you are wrong for the job or areas of inexperience. This could be because you:

- Have not used a computer system or technique
- Have no experience in a certain area
- Were paid more money in previous roles
- Are applying for a more junior role than the last
- Have a long way to travel to the company or may need to relocate

You really need to be hard on yourself with the mind mapping technique helping you identify them. It is best to prepare and practice the answers to these questions well.

Preparing for these questions can be more important than anything else!

Interviewer styles

Challenging interviewer

Most interviewers are pleasant and will ask you questions and in the same way you are trying to impress them, they will be trying to impress you about their job role also.

If applying for a role where you are expected to react quickly to situations you may experience a challenging interviewer.

One interview technique they use is to take things you say and throw them back at you to see how you react to being criticised or challenged. They are trying to see if you get easily flummoxed, possibly even bring out aggression. If not sure how to answer their question, throw it back at them 'Why do you think that?' giving yourself time to reflect.

The technique often involves the interviewer making statements and assumptions aimed at putting you under pressure to see how you react. Alternatively, they could try to get you to agree with statements that will prevent you getting the job. Under pressure, people's answers will often become very honest.

For example, an interviewee who is a manager may state that they have 'an easy going and laid back management style'…The interviewer utilising this technique may comment… 'I'd love to work at your place!'… 'Thank you' says the interviewee… 'Yes, I've always wanted to work in a holiday camp where everyone does what they want…'

Managers are there to achieve results and by negatively interpreting 'easy going and laid back' the interviewer is directly criticising the interviewees management style and undermining its effectiveness. This is why it is important to prepare set answers beforehand, and think about how others can interpret your answers.

If you spot this style of questioning, stay calm and gather your thoughts before answering. Take time out to think, as the interviewer will often speed up the questioning and openly interrupt or change direction quickly. A simple trick is to try and slow down the conversation by providing a more detailed answer. But an experienced interviewer will spot what you are doing and interrupt, focusing you back to the original question.

These really are the most difficult to handle and, no matter what preparation you do, far harder to control. By having thought through your experience, chosen careful examples and prepared for the typical questions, you will be in a far better position than most.

Challenging interviews are not common but be prepared for them especially if applying for a sales / customer focused or senior management role.

Nice and relaxed conversation

Because of their relaxed style the interviewer will often attempt to draw you into agreeing with a line of questioning that undermines your application. They will lead you down a route and draw out information that were you not so at ease may have been withheld.

For example: a sales person may have 50% new business experience and 50% account management. They apply for a new business sales role.

The interviewer will explore whether the interviewee has a preference towards either aspect. Unless the interviewee states 'new business' the interviewer may then focus more upon account management experience and eventually state 'I think your real strength lies in account management, what do you think?' Say 'yes' and you might as well go home as the vacancy is new business. There is nothing wrong with taking the middle ground and stating that you like both aspects, but the role is a new business one.

This leading technique has many forms:

> From what you have told me about your experience, I think you would be better suited to… rather than the role you have applied for.

> Looking at your background, I think you would have trouble adapting to…

What makes people agree with these statements is the approach the interviewer takes, being friendly, personable, very relaxed, and overtly cunning.

Inexperienced interviewers

This makes up the majority. Later we talk about having your own agenda as you may need to focus the interviewer so your experience is drawn out effectively.

Mind games

At the end of your answer there is often a gap where there is silence. People hate this silence and most will start to babble to fill the silence rather than wait to see if the interviewer has a follow on question.

If you have answered the question – SHUT UP.

If the interviewer is not happy with your answer they will ask a follow on question or move on.

Experienced interviewers often use silences to see if you will volunteer additional information which may just undermine your previous answer!

Preparing for the big day

Mental preparation before an interview

The last factor that can really make the difference is how you feel going into an interview. The tricks are:

- Try and chill out the previous evening
- Do not drink too much alcohol as you need to be sharp the next day.
- Go to bed early
- Concentrate on how much preparation you have done and you will realise that you are well prepared for the interview
- If listening to music on the way to your interview play something up beat and to get you feeling good. Do not play soothing music as you need to be on top form and alert

The interview day

Simple tips are:

- Arrive with plenty of time to spare, first impressions really do count
- Take a comfort break, check your appearance and compose yourself
- Sweaty palms often appear due to nervousness. One tip is to place your right palm face downwards on you skirt or trousers, any sweat will then hopefully be absorbed. As the interviewer arrives quickly rub your palm on the material to dry it off. Even if you do not think you suffer from sweaty palms, do this to be on the safe side
- Talk to the receptionist, it allows you to clear your throat and exercise your vocal cords. You can also fill in a few gaps in your research
- When the interviewer arrives, stand-up, shake their hand (firm but not crushing). Look them in the eye and a smile will go down well
- Try to make some small talk, if you can think of something to say, as they lead you through, 'These are nice offices…' etc.
- If you smoke, had garlic the night before, or have halitosis, chew a mint beforehand, but rather than try and swallow the mint as the interviewer arrives, potentially choking, place the mint in the bin beforehand

The interview

The interview starts from the moment you arrive in the building, receptionists often report back to interviewers. Some tips for the interviewee:

- Turn off your mobile phone before you go in
- Don't chew gum in the interview
- If offered a drink, opt for water. You won't be sat trying to sip a hot drink, nor if you drop it on your lap will it stain, a double benefit!

- Be careful with your body language, in particular crossed arms make you look defensive, so place your hands on your lap or hold your drink in one hand
- Smile and be positive in your statements and remarks
- Do not waffle in your answers!
- If, when you talk, you tend to use your hands a lot, be careful not to appear like a windmill
- Do not swing from side to side on your chair
- Keep calm and try not to be flustered. One trick is to remember that everyone has to use the toilet, picture them sitting on it, but don't laugh!
- Do not keep interrupting the interviewer or try to speak over them. Wait until they have finished asking you the question before you answer it
- Do not monopolise the conversation to such an extent that the interviewer is unable to ask questions
- If you are not sure of a question, get the interviewer to repeat it or explain what they mean
- Keep good eye contact (if you are able)
- If you are being interviewed by more than one person, mainly direct your answer to the person asking the question
- Do not mention salary unless they direct a question at you
- By all means ask about the hours of work etc., but put it in such a way that you are not perceived to be a clock watcher
- Be enthusiastic about the role and company
- Remember you are trying to sell yourself
- Make positive reassuring statements to things they say 'That sounds good'
- Firm handshake(s) at the end and a smile
- Be careful if you 'mirror' a person as this technique is easily spotted

Handshakes – a key part to providing a good impression is your handshake. If you are not used to shaking a person's hand practice with someone you know. It is your right hand you use.

Body language

Your interviewer can ascertain so much from your body language. A good video to watch to learn a few tips is on YouTube.

Search under 'Job Interview Body Language' and you will see on page one usually at the top a video produced by 'TheSite.org'. The caption has several pictures of the same man's face.

Hysterical in places, but full of good body language tips.

Questions to ask

We cannot give exact questions to ask as these differ for each application, but relate them to the company, job role and opportunity on offer.

When asked 'do you have any questions?' the interviewer is not testing your memory, but giving you the opportunity to ask them a few questions having just answered many of theirs. So write down a few on a pad before your interview and take them with you.

One area you should try and avoid raising is salary and package details as this can give the wrong impression, unless the interviewer raises it with you.

When asked 'what questions do you have for us?'

Open your folder and ask your pre-prepared questions. If already answered, by the physical process of opening your file, reading the questions, and answering:

> You have actually answered all the questions I was going to ask

They will know that you had prepared some and thought about the interview. This is far better than the usual 'my mind has gone blank; I can't think of any at present...'

One question you MUST ask however is: 'What is the next stage?'

If you don't ask about what happens next it portrays the fact you are not bothered!

If struggling to think of questions, why not ask about:

- Who you will be working with
- Their expectations
- What they would be looking for the person to achieve in the first few months
- What challenges the role has
- Training they will provide
- Why the role is now empty

Have your own interview agenda

We recommend that you go into the interview with your own agenda. Having already taken time to identify your own skill set and how it matches the role, list those areas for reference.

Interviewers often go off at tangents and all your relevant skills and experience may not be drawn out during the interview.

One tip is to have a check list on a pad you take into the interview. You can quickly scan the list to identify any areas you think the interviewer has missed. You do not want to appear to be picking up on a poor interview technique so be careful in your phrasing at this point, one easy way is to blame yourself:

> I noticed in the advertisement that you are looking for someone with... I think we touched earlier on this experience but I do not think I really gave you a full appreciation of my own experience. Are there any more questions you would like to ask me?

The interview close

One of the most common reasons why an individual is rejected is the interviewer was left with the impression that the individual did not really want the job or was not very enthusiastic about it (The Times Survey - 20% of rejections). The interviewer wants, rightly or wrongly, to feel that the person they recruit is enthusiastic about both the role and their company.

So as you finish simply state 'Can I just say that I am very interested in this role...' this will inform the interviewer of your interest and may secure you the job or a second interview. Nerves may have quelled your obvious enthusiasm for the role.

It is a good idea, if you feel confident, to ask an objection handling questions:

> Having met today, are there any areas which give you concerns regarding my experience?

> or

> Do you have any reservations about my ability to do the job?

These questions, if answered honestly by the interviewer, will either reassure you that you have had a good interview, or allow you to try and tackle any doubts or worries they may be having, whilst you are still with them. It may simply give you the opportunity to state that, 'Although I do not have the experience, I believe I have the ability to learn very quickly and would not see that as being a problem.'

In addition, sales people are expected to go further and ask: 'will you be offering me the job?' or 'have I got the job?' or 'when do I start?'

This sounds very pushy, but that is what sales people do for a living. The interviewer wants to see the person close as they would in their role.

It really is important at the end of the interview to provide a positive reinforcement statement such as; 'Thank you for inviting me along today. I must say that I am very interested in the role'. It conveys a true interest and commitment to the role.

Tours of the building

If you are asked if you would like to see the offices or a look round, say yes, it shows interest. But remember not to let your guard down!

Following up interviews

After the interview, should you send a 'thank you for seeing me' email or note? There is no right or wrong answer to this. After you have left the room the interviewer has probably decided whether you are in the mix, or not as the case maybe.

It is a nice gesture to follow up with a quick thank you email, but it probably won't make any difference to the interview outcome.

Watch your online profile

Although not part of your interview preparation, one final area we want to cover is how you are viewed on the internet. With sites such as Facebook and Twitter, what is now emerging is an online profile.

Interviewers may search these sites prior to interviewing a candidate to see what they say about themselves and how they present themselves to the world. Placing the right information on such sites could work for you.

A key site is LinkedIn here you can place a career history/profile. This can be used to really highlight your achievements and background. BUT REMEMBER, identity fraudsters also visit such sites for their own purposes, so be careful what personal information you put on them.

LinkedIn is also now selling access to its profiles to recruiters in the same way a CV database does. A good profile can thus result in employers and agencies contacting your about potential job roles.

Other key sites employers may look at include:

- www.friendsreunited.co.uk
- www.facebook.com
- www.youtube.com
- www.instagram.com

If you are a creative individual you might also wish to upload samples of your work to specialist sites that can provide an advertising platform. You can then include the web addresses on your CV, but please ask other people to look at how your work is displayed on these sites to ensure it looks good before broadcasting the address.

Extra help and support

If you are struggling preparing for your interview or need extra help to in other areas such as CV writing; preparing for a presentation or assessment centre, or effective job hunting; we provide both remote (via Skype and telephone) support; along with 1-2-1 face to face support.

Remote support is available to both UK and International clients and purchased by the hour. 1-2-1 face-to-face support is available in the UK and Republic of Ireland.

For more information please visit: www.job-doctor.com

Or email us at: info@job-doctor.com

Good luck with the interviews!

Disclaimer

Other publications

The only job hunting guide you will ever need…!

The only job hunting guide new graduates need… 2016 edition

www.job-doctor.com

Made in the USA
Charleston, SC
13 February 2016